Grand Canyon
National Park

John Hamilton

Published by ABDO Publishing Company, 4940 Viking Drive, Suite 622, Edina, Minnesota 55435.
Copyright ©2005 by Abdo Consulting Group, Inc. International copyrights reserved in all countries.
No part of this book may be reproduced in any form without written permission from the publisher.
ABDO & Daughters™ is a trademark and logo of ABDO Publishing Company.

Printed in the United States.

Editor: Paul Joseph
Graphic Design: John Hamilton
All photos and illustrations by John Hamilton, except National Park Service, p. 13 (park maps),
p. 15 (rattlesnake and scorpion), p. 16 (Powell), p. 17 (boats), p. 23 (inner canyon) p. 25 (rafters),
p. 26 (squirrel), p. 26 (rim with snow).

Library of Congress Cataloging-in-Publication Data

Hamilton, John, 1959–
    Grand Canyon National Park / John Hamilton.
      p. cm. — (National parks)
    Summary: Discusses the history of this national park, its geological features, human population,
plant and animal life, dangers in the park, and efforts to preserve it.
    Includes bibliographical references and index.
    ISBN 1-59197-426-7
    1. Grand Canyon National Park (Ariz.)—Juvenile literature. [1. Grand Canyon National Park
(Ariz.) 2. National parks and reserves.] I. Title. II. National parks (ABDO Publishing Company)

F788.H245 2005
917.91'32—dc21
                            2003041850

Contents

Hikers enter a tunnel along the South Rim's Bright Angel Trail.

Sunset lights up the walls of the Grand Canyon, as seen from Hopi Point.

Grand Canyon Wonderland

A first-time visit to Arizona's Grand Canyon National Park is a wondrous moment. People are seldom prepared for the spectacle they are about to witness. Photographs simply can't do justice to what most people agree is one of the true wonders of the natural world.

Traveling north out of Flagstaff, Arizona, one crosses flatland that appears as normal and dull as any semi-desert southwestern landscape. The ground rises gently as the plateau stretches to the horizon. Ninety miles (145 km) from Flagstaff, the park entrance finally appears. During the busy summer season, thousands of visitors arrive daily, and the wait to get in can be quite long. Nearly five million tourists flock to the canyon each year.

After passing through the park entrance, the rim of the canyon is nearby, just to the north. The road is lined with pine trees and sagebrush, but still no sign of the canyon. After finding a parking space, visitors hurry to the nearest ledge and then gasp in astonishment. Seeing the Grand Canyon for the first time—or any time—is a humbling experience. The sheer scale of its beauty numbs the mind.

Laid out beyond the rim is a great abyss nearly one mile (1.6 km) deep and in some places 18 miles (29 km) across. The canyon stretches east and west across northwestern Arizona for 277 miles (446 km). The official park boundary holds about 1.2 million acres (485,623 hectares) of protected wilderness. From any vantage point along the rim, you can only see a small fraction of all that is hidden within the canyon walls.

Rising up within this immense gorge are rocky spires, raised plateaus, and deep-walled side canyons. Far below, the Colorado River can be seen as a silvery ribbon winding its way through the depths of the canyon.

Layers of rock range from Kaibab limestone at the top of the canyon to 1.8 billion-year-old gneiss and schist at the bottom. The rocks blaze red, orange, yellow, green, and purple during dramatic canyon sunrises and sunsets. During summer afternoon thunderstorms, shafts of light sometimes pierce the gloom. Rocks struck by dancing sunbeams seem to glow from within. Crowd-pleasing rainbows often appear, straddling canyon walls. In winter, layers of white snow blanket the mesas in hushed silence. There is much to see here, for those willing to take their time and embrace all that Mother Nature reveals.

The Grand Canyon was first seen by Europeans in 1540, but Native Americans have lived in the area for more than 4,000 years. The canyon was set aside as a national park in 1919 so that future generations could enjoy the beauty preserved here.

Most people view the canyon from the South Rim. This part of the national park contains a number of hotels, stores, and visitor centers, even an airport. The less crowded North Rim is only 10 miles (16 km) away across the canyon, but to get there requires a drive of 215 miles (346 km) by car through Arizona's Painted Desert and then across a narrow section of canyon near Lees Ferry to the northeast.

Many people are not content to merely gaze into the canyon from the rim. For these adventurers, there are many paths that descend into the chasm, with such famous trail names as North Kaibab and Bright Angel. At the bottom of the gorge is Phantom Ranch, a park-run overnight resting place for weary hikers. Mule trains and whitewater rafting trips are other ways to explore the canyon.

Millions of visitors flock to see the park's beauty each year.

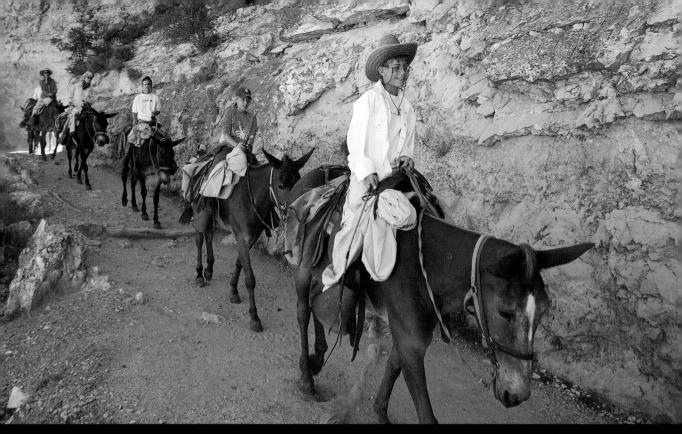

Mule trains (above) are a popular way to explore the inner canyon. Rock formations, such as these seen from the Grand Canyon's South Rim (below), show how climate and erosion have shaped the landscape of the area.

Geology

Anyone who gazes into the Grand Canyon eventually questions how the canyon came to be. How was something this big, so seemingly timeless and majestic, ever created?

Grand Canyon National Park lies on the Colorado Plateau in northwestern Arizona. Millions of years ago the region was at the bottom of a shallow sea. Layers of sedimentary rock, including Kaibab limestone, formed on top of older, harder layers of volcanic rock that were created eons earlier.

Seventy million years ago two tectonic plates collided, causing the western part of North America, including the Colorado Plateau, to rise up over millions of years. The average elevation of the South Rim is 6,800 feet (2,073 m) above sea level. The canyon began forming about five to seven million years ago.

The geological force that cut through the rock was erosion, especially the action of water. As the National Park Service says, "The goal of every raindrop, every rock, every grain of sand is to return to the sea." Water draining off the Rocky Mountains moved westward across the Colorado Plateau, carrying sand and gravel and cutting through ancient layers of rock. Almost half of the canyon, the lower 2,000 feet (610 m), may have been sculpted as recently (in geological terms) as the last 750,00 years.

As the Colorado River cut through the layers, walls collapsed, widening the canyon. Side canyons were created as water flowed down the ever-widening main canyon walls. Erosion from freezing water and plant roots also helped widen the canyon.

The steep canyon walls were created by the forces of erosion.

The walls of the Grand Canyon are made of layers of **sedimentary rock**.

Today we can see many colorful rock layers in the walls of the Grand Canyon. Each layer represents a different kind of rock formed over many geological ages. As the rocks were worn down, softer layers formed slopes, while harder layers formed steep cliffs, giving the canyon a stair step appearance. Almost half of Earth's geological history can be found in the Grand Canyon, which averages about 5,000 feet (1,524 m) deep measured from the South Rim to the Colorado River.

The rock layer at the top, Kaibab limestone, is the youngest. Geologists call this cap rock, and it was formed starting around 270 million years ago. Layers deeper in the canyon were formed longer and longer ago. Traveling down into the canyon is almost like riding in a time machine. Many kinds of fossils can be found in the sedimentary layers of the upper part of the canyon. Shells and trilobites are especially common.

At the very bottom of the canyon are volcanic layers of gneiss and Vishnu schist. Geologists estimate that these rocks are 1.8 billion years old, almost half the age of Earth itself.

The Colorado River is always at work, deepening and widening the Grand Canyon.

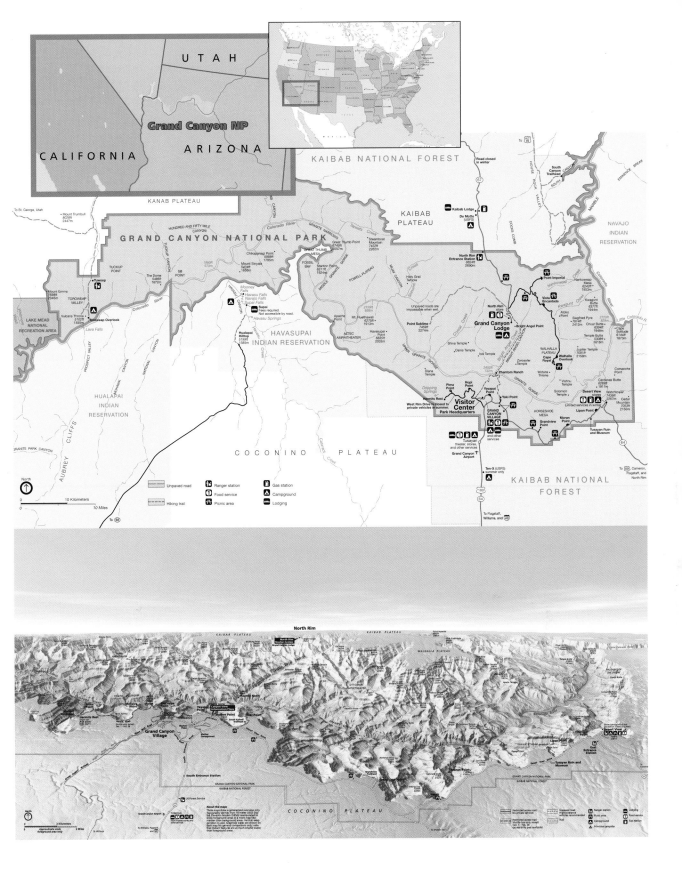

Canyon Ecosystems

Several ecosystems are contained in the Grand Canyon. This biological diversity is due to the extreme changes of elevation found in the park. Scientists have identified seven kinds of life zones on Earth, five of which are in the Grand Canyon. These

include the Lower Sonoran, Upper Sonoran, Transition, Canadian, and Hudsonian life zones. It's like finding plants and wildlife from northern Mexico all the way to southern Canada.

Bighorn sheep

There are more than 350 species of birds in the park. Nearly 100 mammals make their home here, as well as 58 species of reptiles and amphibians. More than 1,500 plants are found in the Grand Canyon. Along the rim of the canyon grow forests of ponderosa pine, pinyon pine, Utah juniper, plus, on the cooler, higher-elevation North Rim, forests of aspen.

Yucca plant

The climate of the park gets hotter and drier the farther one ventures down into the canyon. Most of the inner canyon is desert. The higher-elevation forests give way to cacti and scrub vegetation. A pleasant 70 degree F (21 C) day at the rim may turn into a 100 degree F (38 C) hothouse at the bottom of the chasm.

Pink rattlesnake

Scorpion

The areas along the Colorado River and its tributaries are called riparian (streamside) habitat. Willow, tamarisk, and cottonwood trees can be found here.

Wildlife is abundant in all the canyon's ecosystems. Mule deer are common along the rim. Other large creatures found here include mountain lions, bobcats, coyote, bighorn sheep, and wild turkeys. Many smaller animals make their homes inside the canyon as well, including porcupines, beavers, ringtails (closely related to raccoons), mice, gophers, and rabbits. Lizards and snakes are also common, including pink rattlesnakes, which are found nowhere else in the world.

Raven

People in the Canyon

Native Americans have been living at the Grand Canyon for more than 4,000 years, probably longer. Small, split-twig figurines of animals, created by an early Indian culture called the Anasazi, have been found preserved in caves below the rim of the canyon. The Anasazi, who are now often referred to as the Ancestral Pueblo People, are considered the ancestors of today's Hopi Indians.

In the 1300s, hunter-gatherer Indians moved into the canyon. These included ancestors of today's Hualapai and Havasupai tribes. Around 1400, Navajo Indians settled into the area. They were hunter-gatherers who had learned agriculture from neighboring tribes. Other tribes found in the canyon include the Kaibab-Paiute people. Zuni Indians of New Mexico consider the Grand Canyon their place of origin. Remnants of early Indian cultures can still be found today in the Grand Canyon. These include ancient dwellings, art painted on rock walls, and pottery.

John Wesley Powell in 1873 with Tau-Gu, chief of the Paiute Indians.

John Wesley Powell's boat was equipped with an armchair strapped in the middle.

Early Spanish explorers first came to the area in the 1500s, but it wasn't until 1869 that an organized expedition of white people explored the Grand Canyon. That year, a one-armed Civil War veteran named Major John Wesley Powell set out with nine men and four small, wooden boats and traveled more than 1,000 miles (1,609 km) down the Colorado River. Along the way, these scientist-adventurers explored the inner reaches of the Grand Canyon. Braving monstrous rapids, stifling heat, and lack of food, the expedition emerged three months later with only two boats, and three of their party dead.

Despite the hardships, the expedition learned much about the canyon, which was one of the last places unexplored by whites in the United States. Powell led a second expedition into the canyon, and eventually went on to start the U.S. Geological Survey. Powell was also a strong supporter of Native American rights.

The late 1870s and 1880s saw a boom in mining in the canyon, as prospectors struggled to extract copper and asbestos. At the turn of the century, however, tourism took over as the main industry of the area. Several hotels were built along the South Rim to accommodate the thousands of tourists who began flocking to the canyon to see for their own eyes this newly revealed wonder of nature.

President Theodore Roosevelt was a devoted outdoorsman who had spent time camping and hunting in the canyon area. In 1908, Roosevelt designated the Grand Canyon as a national monument, which gave it partial protection. In 1919, Grand Canyon National Park was created, preserving the area for future generations.

This view from Hopi Point (above, left and right) is most spectacular during sunrise or sunset, when the canyon walls seem to glow from within. The observation station at Yavapai Point (below) can be a good place to escape sudden summer thunderstorms.

The Watchtower at Desert View (below) was built in 1932. Designed by architect Mary Elizabeth Jane Colter, it was built to look like a native Puebloan structure. The 70-foot (21-m) tower is the highest point on the South Rim of the Grand Canyon.

South Rim

The South Rim of the Grand Canyon is by far the most visited. Ninety percent of the five million people who travel to the park each year will spend their time here, gazing at the canyon at overlooks along the rim.

The South Rim is open all year long. It is the most accessible part of the park. The main park visitor center is located here. There are many hotel rooms available, some right on the ledge of the canyon. Camping is also popular. In winter, the park is less crowded, but there is often snow to contend with.

Most of the South Rim's development is contained in Canyon Village, near the park's south entrance. Shuttle busses, which cut down on traffic, ferry visitors through the village and along Hermit Road. The eight-mile (13 km) roadway contains several scenic vistas, including breathtaking Hopi Point. This promontory juts out into the canyon for incredible views, especially at dusk or dawn. For walkers, the Rim Trail follows close to the edge of the canyon for several miles.

Private vehicles are allowed on Desert View Drive, which winds along the canyon rim until reaching the east park entrance, about 26 miles (42 km) away.

There are many spots along the South Rim to stop and admire the scenery, which changes constantly as the sun and the weather cycle through the day.

Utah juniper trees (above) require very little water to survive, which allows them to thrive in the desert climate of the South Rim. Pinon pines, cacti, and yucca plants are also common. Sunset on the South Rim (below) is a sight most people never forget.

The Inner Canyon

Seeing the Grand Canyon from a scenic vista along the rim is a wonderful experience, but many people want more. The Inner Canyon includes anything below the rim. It is open to hikers, mule riders, and river rafters.

The majority of the park's 1.2 million acres (485,623 hectares) are inaccessible to people. But a network of trails leads down into the canyon, with scenery quite different from the rim. Hikers feel small and insignificant as the canyon walls tower over them.

A mule train starts down Bright Angel Trail, heading for Phantom Ranch at the bottom of the Grand Canyon.

The **Colorado River** winds through the bottom of the canyon.

Hiking into the canyon can be very challenging. Many people have trouble dealing with the heat and high altitude. Most often, hikers are lulled into believing it is an easy stroll. That is, until it is time to hike back out. Then they realize that hiking the Grand Canyon is like mountain climbing in reverse. The climb out can be very strenuous, especially during the heat of midday, or if one hasn't packed in enough water. Dehydration is a very real danger in the park. So are accidental falls when hikers slip too close to the edge of cliffs.

From the South Rim, a trip to the bottom of the canyon is eight miles (13 km) down the Bright Angel Trail, or 6.5 miles (10.5 km) down the South Kaibab Trail, which is steeper but shorter. A 21-mile (34 km) rim-to-rim trip takes most hikers at least two days to accomplish, with a stop at Phantom Ranch at the bottom of the canyon. For an easier trip into the canyon, some people ride mules.

You don't have to go all the way to the bottom to enjoy an Inner Canyon hike. Several trails, especially Bright Angel, are well suited for day hiking. Careful preparation is still required, however. Carry enough water, and check for weather conditions. Late afternoon thunderstorms can sneak up on hikers. Lightning is a common danger in the park.

Some visitors prefer to see the Grand Canyon at river level. Colorado River rafting trips are a once-in-a-lifetime adventure for many people. Trips usually take from one to two weeks to float down the length of the canyon. Calm sections of water let visitors gaze in wonder as soaring cliffs loom overhead. But at many points, the river rages through violent rapids, challenging even the most experienced river guides. Most guided raft tours stop along the way so visitors can explore side canyons, waterfalls, and Native American ruins.

A cowboy prepares a mule train for a trip into the canyon.

The endangered California condor (above) has a wing span up to 9.5 feet (2.9 m). In the late 1990's, condors were successfully reintroduced into the Grand Canyon ecosystem. River rafters (below) float down the Colorado River.

North Rim

The Grand Canyon's North Rim is higher than the South Rim, with an average elevation of 8,000 feet (2,438 m) above sea level. This part of the park is much less crowded, mainly because it is less accessible. It is a five-hour drive by car from the South Rim.

The climate is different here, with more water than the desert South Rim. The view from the North Rim is also different. The canyon walls seem to project outward. There isn't as much of a feeling of dropping into an abyss.

The North Rim is only open from mid May to mid October. During the winter months snow closes the road leading to the rim. During summer, tourists usually stop at the park visitor center and the Grand Canyon Lodge. In the lodge dining room, you can eat a meal while gazing out into the canyon, one of the best views of any restaurant in the world.

There are several places to hike along the North Rim, including Point Imperial and Cape Royal. These are reached by a winding road that leads through ponderosa pine forests filled with wildlife, including Kaibab squirrels, which are found only here on the Kaibab Plateau.

The North Rim appeals to people who want to see the Grand Canyon, yet escape the crowds that seem to increase every year on the South Rim. It is a good place to imagine what the canyon must have been like before widespread tourism tainted the wilderness experience.

The Kaibab squirrel is known for its long, tassel-shaped ears. It is also called Albert's squirrel.

Sunset at Cape Royal (above) on the North Rim. The large rock formation on the right is called Wotans Throne. In the winter, the North Rim receives much more snow than the other side of the canyon (below).

Future Challenges

In 1919, the year that the Grand Canyon became a national park, fewer than 45,000 people visited the area. Today, nearly five million people come every year. This crush of civilization has affected the park in many ways.

On peak summer days, tourists jostle with each other for parking spaces, hotel rooms, and viewing spots along the rim. The National Park Service restricted private vehicle access to many of the roads in Canyon Village, using instead a system of shuttle busses. This has helped cut down automobile congestion, but overcrowding persists.

Air pollution is a growing threat to the Grand Canyon. Pollution from metropolitan areas and coal-fired power plants often drifts into the canyon, obscuring visibility by as much as 30 percent below natural levels. Water pollution from cattle and human waste has found its way into canyon streams. Non-native animals and plants, introduced by people, crowd out native species as they compete for precious water and food. In 1963, the Glen Canyon Dam was constructed upstream on the Colorado River. The dam changed the flow of the river, and altered the riparian and aquatic ecosystems in the park.

Many people today are working hard to preserve the Grand Canyon. Pest management techniques are eliminating many non-native plants and animals. Nearby power plants have installed special equipment called scrubbers to reduce air pollution. Native American tribes and environmental groups have partnered to find ways for Glen Canyon Dam to have less of an impact on the Inner Canyon's ecosystem.

President Theodore Roosevelt loved the Grand Canyon, and his advice to future generations was simple: "The ages have been at work on it and man can only mar it. What you can do is to keep it for your children, your children's children, and for all who come after you."

Sunset at Powell Point on the Grand Canyon's South Rim

Glossary

Ecosystem

A biological community of animals, plants, and bacteria, all of whom live together in the same physical or chemical environment.

Federal lands

Much of America's land, especially in the western part of the country, is maintained by the United States federal government. These are public lands owned by all U.S. citizens. There are many kinds of federal lands. National parks, like Grand Canyon, are federal lands that are set aside so that they can be preserved. Other federal lands, such as national forests or national grasslands, are used in many different ways, including logging, ranching, and mining. Much of the land surrounding the Grand Canyon is maintained by the government, including several national forests and wildlife refuges.

Forest Service

The United States Department of Agriculture (USDA) Forest Service was started in 1905 to manage public lands in national forests and grasslands. The Forest Service today oversees an area of 191 million acres (77.3 million hectares), which is an amount of land about the same size as Texas. In addition to protecting and managing America's public lands, the Forest Service also conducts forestry research and helps many state government and private forestry programs.

Geological Survey

The United States Geological Survey was created in 1879. It is an independent science agency that is part of the Department of the Interior. It researches and collects facts about the land of the United States, giving us a better understanding of our natural resources.